Travel English in Action

役に立つ旅行英語

Tyler Burden
Tsuyoshi Chiba
Yau-Sin Cheng
Kiyoshi Fukasawa
Mariko Nagahama
Takamasa Fukuoka

NAN'UN-DO

Travel English in Action

このテキストの音声を無料で視聴（ストリーミング）・ダウンロードできます。自習用音声としてご活用ください。
以下のサイトにアクセスしてテキスト番号で検索してください。

https://nanun-do.com テキスト番号 [**512149**]

※ 無線 LAN（WiFi）に接続してのご利用を推奨いたします。

※ 音声ダウンロードは Zip ファイルでの提供になります。
お使いの機器によっては別途ソフトウェア（アプリケーション）の導入が必要となります。

Travel English in Action 音声ダウンロードページは
左記の QR コードからもご利用になれます。

Read by

Shizuka Anderson

Guy Perryman

教科書の構成

この教科書は旅行英語についての身近な話題をテーマとしています。

I. Before You Listen

単語の意味を確認する問題です。取り上げられている単語は、次の II. Listening Practice に出てくる単語が選択されています。内容把握のためにもキーワードの意味をよく理解して下さい。

II. Listening Practice

英会話とリスニングの学習を行います。その上で、質問に対する最も適切な答えを選びます。

III. Fill in the Gaps

II. の英会話を再度リスニング学習して空所に適切な単語を記入します。

IV. Everyday English Phrases

II. の英会話に既出の表現のほか、ユニットごとのテーマに関連し参考になる英語表現のリスニング学習を行います。その上で、ディクテーション（全文書き取り）学習を行います。

V. Incomplete Sentences

各ユニットのテーマに沿った文法・語彙・表現の練習問題です。空所補充の適語選択で、2択、4択、語群内選択の3パターンが出題されています。

VI. Making Sentences

文整序の練習問題です。問題は II. の英会話の内容に準拠しており、日本文が表示されています。

Contents

Unit 1

Summer Holiday Plans

I. Before You Listen

Match the words on the left with their definitions on the right. If you don't know a word's meaning, take a guess.

1. recommend ( ) (A) well known by many people
2. tournament ( ) (B) the area outside cities and towns
3. famous ( ) (C) to advise someone to do something
4. love ( ) (D) impressive in style and size
5. visit ( ) (E) the natural features of a particular place
6. countryside ( ) (F) a series of competitions in a game or sport
7. stately ( ) (G) to really enjoy doing something
8. scenery ( ) (H) to go and spend time in a place or with someone

II. Listening Practice

 02

Kanako is talking to her British friend James. Listen to their conversation and then answer the questions that follow.

Kanako: Hi, James. I'm planning to go to the UK this summer. Can I ask you a few questions about the UK?

James: Sure, Kanako. What would you like to know?

Kanako: I'm planning to go for two weeks, and I was wondering where you recommend I go.

James: Well, that depends on what you want to do. But I think you should spend most of your time in London—one week, perhaps—because there are so many great things to do there. You like tennis, don't you?

Kanako: I sure do.

James: Well, you could go to Wimbledon and watch the tennis tournament there. It's quite easy to get tickets.

Kanako: That would be wonderful!

James: Oh, and I know you're a big music fan, too. Well, there's an area called Camden in northwest London that is famous for live music. I'm sure you'd love it there.

Kanako: Great! So, if I spend one week in London, where should I go for the other week?

James: I think you should visit some of our beautiful national parks. The countryside in the UK is beautiful. One place I especially recommend is the Peak District. It has amazing scenery and a beautiful old stately home.

Kanako: Excuse me, but what is a "stately home"?

James: It's a large historical house and park where rich and important people once lived.

Kanako: Right. I think I've seen one on TV.

James: I also recommend Devon and Dartmoor National Park. The scenery is awesome, and you can go on some great walks and stop in at some beautiful old pubs.

1. Which country is Kanako planning to visit?
   (A) The US
   (B) Canada
   (C) Australia
   (D) The UK

2. How does James recommend that Kanako spend her time?
   (A) Two weeks in the city
   (B) One week in the city and one week in the countryside
   (C) Two weeks in the countryside and one week in the city
   (D) Two weeks in the countryside

3. What does James say is special about Camden?
   (A) It's a good place to see live music.
   (B) It's a good place to watch tennis.
   (C) It has a lot of nice restaurants.
   (D) It's a good place to go shopping.

4. Why does James recommend Devon?
   (A) For the countryside and the tennis
   (B) For the countryside and the pubs
   (C) For the great restaurants and art exhibitions
   (D) For the live music and the tennis tournament

III. Fill in the Gaps

As you listen to the conversation again, fill in each gap with the correct word.

Kanako: Hi, James. I'm planning to go to the UK this summer. Can I ask you a few questions about the UK?

James: Sure, Kanako. What would you like to know?

Kanako: I'm planning to go for two weeks, and I was wondering where you recommend I go.

James: Well, that 1)_____ 2)_____ what you want to do. But I think you should 3)_____ most of your time in London—one week, perhaps—because there are so many great things to do there. You like tennis, don't you?

Kanako: I sure do.

James: Well, you could go to Wimbledon and watch the tennis tournament there. It's quite easy to get 4)_____.

Kanako: That would be wonderful!

James: Oh, and I know you're a big music fan, too. Well, there's an 5)_____ called Camden in northwest London that is 6)_____ for live music. I'm sure you'd love it there.

Kanako: Great! So, if I spend one week in London, where should I go for the other week?

James: I think you should 7)_____ some of our beautiful national parks. The countryside in the UK is beautiful. One place I especially recommend is the Peak District. It has amazing 8)_____ and a beautiful old stately home.

Kanako: Excuse me, but what is a "stately home"?

James: It's a large historical 9)_____ and park where rich and important people once lived.

Kanako: Right. I think I've seen one on TV.

James: I also recommend Devon and Dartmoor National Park. The scenery is awesome. You can go on some great walks and stop in at some beautiful old pubs.

Ⅳ. Everyday English Phrases

Listen to the audio and write what you hear.

1. ....

2. ....

3. ....

4. ....

Ⅴ. Incomplete Sentences

Choose the word from the box that best completes each sentence below.

1. These trips are mostly just 30 minutes' (   ) an hour's drive from the hotel.

2. Sumida Ward in Tokyo is benefiting (   ) the greater tourism that Tokyo Skytree has attracted.

3. Domestic travel has enormous potential, racking (   ) sales worth 22 trillion yen in 2019.

4. Now is the time to focus (   ) the needs of domestic tourists.

5. Student volunteers typically increase in number (   ) the summer holiday period.

(A) up	(B) off	(C) with	(D) to	(E) over
(F) on	(G) by	(H) during	(I) from	(J) of

Ⅵ. Making Sentences

Unscramble the words in the parentheses to make complete English sentences.

1. 私はこの夏、欧州に行く計画をしています。

   I'm _____ .

   (go, this, to, planning, to, Europe, summer)

2. 1週間ロンドンに滞在して、それからイギリスのカントリーサイドに行くかもしれません。

   I will stay in London for a week, and then I _____ .

   (think, the, go, UK, will, I, to, countryside)

3. あなたのホームタウンで見る価値のある古くて重要な場所や建物はありますか？

   Are there _____ in your hometown?

   (worth, buildings, important, old, any, seeing)

4. 2週間の休暇にいくら持って行ったらよいかアドバイスしてもらえますか？

   _____ to bring for a two-week vacation?

   (how, advise, you, me, do, much, money)

5. 2年ぶりに海外旅行をすることができました。

   I was able to travel abroad _____ .

   (time, years, in, for, the, two, first)

Coffee Break

英語習得時間について

「日本人は、中学、高校と6年間も勉強しているのになぜ英語ができないのか」と言われて久しいですが、果たして「6年間も」という表現は適切でしょうか。というのも英語習得には約3000時間が必要と言われていますが、日本人の英語学習時間は塾などを除くと中学、高校で1000時間超に過ぎないからです（最近では小学校から英語に触れる機会が増えました）。仮に一日5時間の英語学習を毎日続けたとしましょう。この1000時間は200日、英語習得に必要な3000時間は600日（2年かかりません）しかありません。つまり、6年間における日本人の英語学習時間は圧倒的に足りないのです。もちろん、日本人の英語力不足の要因は、これまでの英語教育が文法中心であり、インプットに比べてアウトプットが極端に不足しているという側面も大きいのですが、英語力をしっかり身につけるには、普段からもっと英語に触れる機会を増やす必要があるということです。

Unit 2 Online Booking

I. Before You Listen

Match the words on the left with their definitions on the right. If you don't know a word's meaning, take a guess.

1. accommodation ( )
2. terrible   ( )
3. reasonable   ( )
4. available   ( )
5. review   ( )
6. dirty   ( )
7. rent   ( )
8. sound   ( )

(A) an article about a book, movie, play, or some leisure activity

(B) to pay money to use or borrow something

(C) to seem or appear good or bad, boring or exciting, etc.

(D) a room in a hotel or other place where you stay on vacation

(E) not costing a lot of money; cheap

(F) able to be used; open; on hand

(G) not clean

(H) very bad; not good; awful

II. Listening Practice

Listen to the conversation below about booking accommodation and answer the questions that follow.

James: Hi, Kanako. What are you up to?

Kanako: I'm looking for accommodation for my trip to London next month.

James: I see. What websites are you using?

Kanako: This one's called hotellondon.com. I enter my dates and the area I want to stay in, and it gives me a list of hotels and their prices.

James: Right. So, have you found anywhere that you like?

Kanako: Well, not really. They are all either too expensive or too far away. There are some hotels still available near the city center, but they get terrible reviews.

James: Reviews?

Kanako: Yes. The website shows reviews from guests who have used the hotel in the past. This one here—the Thames River Hotel—gets only one out of five stars because the guest says it's dirty and the air conditioning doesn't work.

James: Oh dear! That doesn't sound at all nice. Have you tried roomrental. com?

Kanako: No, I haven't. What's that?

James: It's a website that helps you find rooms to rent for a short stay. I hear that the rooms are reasonable.

Kanako: That sounds interesting. I'll give it a try.

1. Where is Kanako going?
   (A) London
   (B) New York
   (C) Amsterdam
   (D) Paris

2. How is Kanako getting information about places to stay?
   (A) By talking to travel agents
   (B) By searching the Internet
   (C) By reading a guidebook
   (D) By calling some hotels

3. Why is The Thames River Hotel not a good place to stay?
   (A) Because it's not clean and some of its facilities are broken.
   (B) Because it's far from the city center and very expensive.
   (C) Because it is quite reasonable.
   (D) Because it is no longer available.

4. What is the good point about the roomrental.com website that is mentioned?
   (A) It has fair-price accommodation.
   (B) It gets good reviews.
   (C) It is well known.
   (D) It offers only the best hotels.

Ⅲ. Fill in the Gaps

As you listen to the conversation again, fill in each gap with the correct word.

James: Hi, Kanako. What are you up to?

Kanako: I'm 1)_____ 2)_____ accommodation for my trip to London next month.

James: I see. What websites are you using?

Kanako: This one's called hotellondon.com. I enter my dates and the area I want to 3)_____ in, and it gives me a list of hotels and their 4)_____.

James: Right. So, have you found anywhere that you like?

Kanako: Well, not really. They are all either too expensive or too far away. There are some hotels still available near the city 5)_____, but they get terrible 6)_____.

James: Reviews?

Kanako: Yes. The website shows reviews from 7)_____ who have used the hotel in the past. This one here—the Thames River Hotel—gets only one out of five stars because the guest says it's expensive and the air conditioning doesn't 8)_____.

James: Oh dear! That doesn't sound at all nice. Have you tried roomrental. com?

Kanako: No, I haven't. What's that?

James: It's a website that helps you find rooms to rent for a short stay. I hear that the rooms are reasonable.

Kanako: That sounds interesting. I'll give it a 9)_____.

IV. Everyday English Phrases

Listen to the audio and write what you hear.

1. ....

2. ....

3. ....

4. ....

V. Incomplete Sentences

Choose the word in the parentheses that best completes each sentence below.

1. Our new system is an all-in-one online booking method (with / on) a free and easy-to-use plug-in.

2. Booking for the musical must be made at least a month (in / at) advance.

3. To start, simply click (in / on) the booking button.

4. This saves users from having to create a separate log-in (for / into) booking.

5. Creating an online profile is optional, but (with / by) doing so, you will simplify the booking process.

VI. Making Sentences

Unscramble the words in the parentheses to make complete English sentences.

1. ちょうどいま、新しいウェブサイトで旅行の宿泊先を探しているところです。

   Right now, I'm ——————————————————— a new website.

   (looking, trip, on, for, for, my, accommodation)

2. 宿泊したい日付と場所を入力すると、ウェブサイトがホテルのリストを掲示します。

   I enter my dates and ———————————————, and the website gives me a list of hotels.

   (stay, want, the, to, I, in, area)

3. 熱海の手頃な値段のホテルについて情報を教えてもらえますか？

   Would you mind giving

   in Atami?

   (about, me, some, priced, reasonably, hotels, information)

4. 中央ターミナル駅の近くにホテルを見つけてもらえるとありがたいです。

   It'd be great ——————————————— near the central terminal station.

   (find, you, me, a, could, hotel, if)

5. ホリデイ・インに空室があるようです。予約しましょうか？

   —————————————————————— at the Holiday Inn.

   Would you like me to make a reservation for you?

   (seem, some, available, there, to, rooms, be)

Coffee Break

英語での講義について

英語圏の大学だけでなく、EUや東南アジアの大学における多くの講義は、英語で行われていることを知っていますか？現在、世界では、高等教育は英語で受けるというのがグローバルスタンダードになりつつあります。日本でも近年、全講義を英語で行う大学・学部が増えてきましたが、決して多いとは言えません。いまだ希少な存在です。その理由は、日本で英語で講義を行うことができる教授が少ないことと講義を受ける学生の英語力不足にあると言っても過言ではありません（英語で講義を受けるには、最低でも TOEFL 80 が必要）。母語である日本語で大学の講義を受け、知識・教養を身につけることができることは、確かに大きなアドバンテージです。しかし、現在、最先端研究の多くは英語で行われ、英語で発表され、様々な国の人たちによって英語で議論されています。これらの研究を日本語に訳し、訳された日本語を英語に訳していては、世界の潮流から遅れてしまいます。

In an Airplane

I. Before You Listen

Match the words on the left with their definitions on the right. If you don't know a word's meaning, take a guess.

1. press   ( )   (A) to arrive at an airport on a flight
2. compartment ( )   (B) to make an official statement about how much money or what things you have with you
3. land   ( )   (C) in a moment; soon; before long
4. assistance   ( )   (D) to push something like an elevator button
5. declare   ( )   (E) to be concerned or unhappy about something
6. worry   ( )   (F) the people who work for a company or other organization
7. staff   ( )   (G) a smaller enclosed space inside something larger
8. shortly   ( )   (H) help

II. Listening Practice

Kanako is flying on a plane to the UK and talking to a flight attendant. Listen to their conversation and then answer the questions that follow.

Attendant: You pressed the button for assistance. Can I help you?

Kanako: Yes, thank you. I'm feeling a little chilly. May I get a blanket, please?

Attendant: There's one in your overhead compartment. Let me get it down for you. Here you are.

Kanako: Thanks a lot. Oh, and um, … do you have a landing card for me to fill out? I'd like to fill it out before we land at Heathrow.

Attendant: Actually, visitors to the UK don't need to fill out landing cards anymore.

Kanako: Really? Why's that?

Attendant: The government decided it was unnecessary to make everyone fill out a form.

Kanako: I didn't know that. So, what about the customs declaration form?

Attendant: You don't have to fill out one of those, either.

Kanako: Is that so? So how do I know if I need to declare something?

Attendant: If you are worried about it, you can ask the customs staff at the airport.

Kanako: OK, thanks. By the way, I ordered a special meal.

Attendant: Yes, that's right. It was a vegetarian meal, wasn't it?

Kanako: That's right.

Attendant: We'll be serving you shortly.

Kanako: Great. Thanks.

1. What does the flight attendant give Kanako?
   (A) A blanket
   (B) A drink
   (C) A customs declaration form
   (D) A headset

2. Why is Kanako surprised?
   (A) Because the flight attendant forgot her special meal.
   (B) Because it was so chilly inside the plane.
   (C) Because she doesn't have to fill out a landing card.
   (D) Because she has nothing to declare.

3. What kind of meal did Kanako order?
   (A) Low-calorie
   (B) Child's
   (C) Japanese
   (D) Vegetarian

4. What will Kanako do soon?
   (A) Land at Heathrow
   (B) Fill out the landing card
   (C) Fill out the customs declaration form
   (D) Eat a meal

Ⅲ. Fill in the Gaps

As you listen to the conversation again, fill in each gap with the correct word.

Attendant: You pressed the button for 1)_____. Can I help you?

Kanako: Yes, thank you. I'm feeling a little chilly. May I get a blanket, please?

Attendant: There's one in your 2)_____ 3)_____. Let me get it down for you. Here you are.

Kanako: Thanks a lot. Oh and um, ... do you have a landing card for me to 4)_____ 5)_____? I'd like to fill it out before we 6)_____ at Heathrow.

Attendant: Actually, visitors to the UK don't need to fill out landing cards anymore.

Kanako: Really? Why's that?

Attendant: The 7)_____ decided it was unnecessary to make everyone fill out a form.

Kanako: I didn't know that. So, what about the customs declaration 8)_____?

Attendant: You don't have to fill out one of those, either.

Kanako: Is that so? So how do I know if I need to declare something?

Attendant: If you are worried about it, you can ask the customs staff at the airport.

Kanako: OK, thanks. 9)_____ 10)_____ 11)_____, I ordered a special meal.

Attendant: Yes, that's right. It was a vegetarian meal, wasn't it?

Kanako: That's right.

Attendant: We'll be 12)_____ you shortly.

Kanako: Great. Thanks.

IV. Everyday English Phrases

 07

Listen to the audio and write what you hear.

1. ....

2. ....

3. ....

4. ....

V. Incomplete Sentences

Choose the word that best completes each sentence below.

1. If the captain gets sick, the co-pilot can take (   ).

    (A) over   (B) on   (C) out   (D) in

2. We are next in line to take (   ) on Runway 5.

    (A) in   (B) down   (C) for   (D) off

3. Being so tall, you might be more comfortable (   ) an aisle seat.

    (A) on   (B) by   (C) in   (D) among

4. This inflight meal is designed (   ) passengers who want to reduce their calorie intake.

    (A) for   (B) in   (C) from   (D) up

5. I got really lucky. I had an economy-seat ticket, but the airline overbooked, so they ended (   ) seating me in first class.

    (A) with   (B) up   (C) on   (D) of

VI. Making Sentences

Unscramble the words in the parentheses to make complete English sentences.

1. 少し寒いのですが、もう1枚毛布をもらえますか。

   I'm feeling a little chilly. _____ ?

   (blanket, I, may, have, another)

2. あの通路側の座席に移っていいですか？

   May _____ ?

   (move, seat, I, that, aisle, to)

3. 座席を倒してもいいですか？

   Do you _____ ?

   (seat, mind, I, if, my, lean, back)

4. どんな飲み物がありますか？アルコール飲料は有料ですか？

   What drinks do you have? Is _____ ?

   (for, a, liquor, charge, there)

5. すみません、食事のトレイを下げてもらえますか？

   Excuse me. Can _____ , please?

   (take, tray, you, my, away)

Coffee Break

英語人口について

現代社会において、英語はリンガ・フランカとしての地位を確立しましたが、果たして世界で英語を話す人たちはいったいどのくらい存在するのでしょうか。一説によると約15億人と言われています。世界の人口は、約80億人ですので、世界の約20％が英語を話していることになります。そして、それらの約25％が英語圏の人たちであり、残りの約75％が皆さんと同じ、第二言語として英語を話している人たちになります。英語が得意な人がいれば、不得意な人もいるでしょう。好きな人もいれば嫌いな人もいるでしょう。しかし、これらの数字は、世界において英語がもはやそのような次元のものではなく、「英語を使えて当たり前、英語"ぐらい"」になったことを示唆しています。つまり、世界では母語に加えて英語を使えることは、決して特別なことではないということです。実際、EUでは、母語と英語に加えて、その他言語を加えたトリリンガル（三言語話者）が増えてきています。

Unit 4 · Exchanging Money

I. Before You Listen

Match the words on the left with their definitions on the right. If you don't know a word's meaning, take a guess.

1. currency ( )   (A) a piece of paper money
2. credit ( )   (B) to make someone pay money for a service
3. rate ( )   (C) percentage of money paid to agents, salespeople, etc.
4. search ( )   (D) the value of a coin, paper money, or stamp
5. commission ( )   (E) being able to buy or obtain things before paying for them
6. charge ( )   (F) a set price for a good or service
7. denomination ( )   (G) to look for someone or something
8. note ( )   (H) the type of money that a particular country uses

II. Listening Practice

Kanako is at Heathrow Airport in London. She talks to her friend Mike about exchanging money and then talks to a cashier at a money exchange. Listen to the conversations and answer the questions that follow.

Kanako: Mike, I need to change some money. I don't have any UK currency at all.

Mike: Sure, but the exchange rate here in this airport won't be very good. You'd be better off using an ATM.

Kanako: Right, but my credit card is in the bottom of my suitcase somewhere, and I don't want to search for it now. I only want to change a little money.

Mike: You'll have to use one of the money changers here, then. That one over there seems to have a good exchange rate.

Kanako: OK, I'll try that one. Thanks.

(At the money exchange)

Kanako: Err.. excuse me. I'd like to change some Japanese yen into British pounds. How much commission do you charge?

Cashier: We don't charge any commission.

Kanako: I see. So, can you tell me how many British pounds I can get for 40,000 Japanese yen?

Cashier: 40,000 Japanese yen? That will be three hundred and two pounds and fifty pence.

Kanako: OK. Here's my yen.

Cashier: May I see your passport, please?

Kanako: Yes, sure. Here you are.

Cashier: Thanks. Would you like your pounds in any special denominations?

Kanako: Pardon me?

Cashier: How would you like your money? In tens, twenties, or fifty-pound notes?

Kanako: Oh, I see. May I have it in twenties and tens, please?

Cashier: Certainly.

1. How much UK money does Kanako have with her when she arrives at the airport?
   (A) None
   (B) 20 pounds
   (C) 300 pounds
   (D) 40,000 pounds

2. What is Mike's advice about exchanging money at the airport?
   (A) Use an ATM.
   (B) Buy traveler's checks.
   (C) Go to a bank.
   (D) Never use an airport money changer.

3. Why doesn't Kanako use her credit card at the airport?
   (A) Because she forgot to bring it.
   (B) Because UK ATMs won't accept it.
   (C) Because it's too expensive to use.
   (D) Because it's too much trouble to open her suitcase.

4. What does Kanako show the money changer?
   (A) Her driver's license
   (B) Her credit card
   (C) Her passport
   (D) Her ticket

5. How much money does Kanako exchange?
   (A) 400 yen
   (B) 4,000 yen
   (C) 40,000 yen
   (D) 400,000 yen

Ⅲ. Fill in the Gaps

As you listen to the conversation again, fill in each gap with the correct word.

Kanako: Mike, I need to 1)_____ some money. I don't have any UK currency at all.

Mike: Sure, but the 2)_____ 3)_____ here in this airport won't be very good. You'd be better off using an 4)_____.

Kanako: Right, but my 5)_____ 6)_____ is in the bottom of my suitcase somewhere, and I don't want to search for it now. I only want to change a little money.

Mike: You'll have to use one of the money changers here, then. That one over there seems to have a good exchange rate.

Kanako: OK, I'll try that one. Thanks.

(At the money exchange)

Kanako: Err.., excuse me. I'd like to change some Japanese yen into British pounds. How much 7)_____ do you 8)_____?

Cashier: We don't charge any commission.

Kanako: I see. So, can you tell me how many British pounds I can get for 40,000 Japanese yen?

Cashier: 40,000 Japanese yen? That will be three hundred and two pounds and fifty pence.

Kanako: OK. Here's my yen.

Cashier: May I see your passport?

Kanako: Yes, sure. Here you are.

Cashier: Thanks. Would you like your pounds in any special 9)_____?

Kanako: Pardon me?

Cashier: How would you like your money? In tens, twenties, or fifty-pound 10)_____?

Kanako: Oh I see. Can I have it in twenties and tens please.

Cashier: Certainly.

IV. Everyday English Phrases

 09

Listen to the audio and write what you hear.

1. ....

2. ....

3. ....

4. ....

V. Incomplete Sentences

Choose the word or phrase in the parentheses that best completes each sentence below.

1. Overseas travelers often (get excited at / worry about) high fees and unfair exchange rates.

2. Many tourists in Japan mention the challenges they (encounter / develop) with foreign currency exchange.

3. Since many smaller shops or restaurants in Japan (don't accept / have no) credit cards, always be sure to have some cash on you.

4. There are some 2,000-yen notes in circulation in Japan that can be (refused for / confused with) 1,000-yen notes.

5. When entering or leaving Japan, a customs declaration is (accepted / required) if you are carrying more than one million yen in cash, checks, traveler's checks, securities, etc.

VI. Making Sentences

Unscramble the words in the parentheses to make complete English sentences.

1. 日本円をアメリカドルに両替してもらえますか？

   _____?

   (change, yen, into, dollars, you, can, Japanese, US)

2. 20ドル紙幣を3枚、10ドル紙幣を3枚、残りは小銭でお願いします。

   I'd like _____ in small bills, please.

   (three, three, and, rest, twenties, tens, the)

3. イギリスの紙幣と硬貨は何種類ありますか？

   How _____ coins are there?

   (banknotes, different, of, types, and, British, many)

4. 4桁の暗証番号を入れて、エンターキーを押して下さい。

   Enter your _____.

   (press, PIN, enter, then, 4-Digit, key, the)

5. 現金はチップや少額の買い物に用いる分があればいいです。

   Cash should _____.

   (tips, used, small, and, be, for, purchases)

Coffee Break

生きた例文

皆さんは単語や熟語をどのように覚えていますか。英単語や熟語を見て日本語に訳す、あるいは、日本語から英単語や熟語を言えるようにする、といった方法をとっている人が多いのではないでしょうか。しかし、こうした方法だと、例えば、must や have to は両方ともに「～しなければならない」と訳され、これらの違いを理解できません（must は話し手の主観的な理由や強制、have to は客観的な状況や背景によって生じる義務）、また、should を「～をすべきである」、had better を「～した方が良い」と覚えていると、目上の人に何か提案しようとした時に、should ではなく had better を使ってしまうかもしれません。こうした違いをしっかり理解するのは、英単語や熟語と日本語を対にして覚えるのではなく、生きた文章の中で覚えることが必要です。英単語帳に載っている例文も良いですが、英字新聞・雑誌、ネットによる英文記事等にできるだけ多く触れ、どのような場面でどのような単語や熟語が使われているかを確認しながら覚えると良いでしょう。

Unit 5 — At the Accommodation

I. Before You Listen

Match the words on the left with their definitions on the right. If you don't know a word's meaning, take a guess.

1. landlord   ( )   (A) the distance in a city from one street to the next
2. stay   ( )   (B) the owner of a building
3. rule   ( )   (C) to not see, hear, or notice something
4. selection   ( )   (D) an item of electrical equipment used in the home
5. block   ( )   (E) normal; usual; average
6. miss   ( )   (F) a guide for correct behavior; standard; order
7. regular   ( )   (G) choice of different things
8. appliance   ( )   (H) living somewhere for a short time

II. Listening Practice

Kanako is now in London and checking in to her accommodation. Listen to the conversation and answer the questions that follow.

Julie: Hi! Are you Kanako? I'm Julie, the host of the short-stay room for rent that you booked.

Kanako: Yes, I'm Kanako. Hello, Julie. Pleased to meet you.

Julie: Let me take you to the room. It's not far from here.

Kanako: Thanks.

Julie: Do you have any questions?

Kanako: Err...yes. I read about the room on the website, but I didn't see many rules mentioned. It said, "No pets" and "No parties." Are there any other rules?

Julie: Yes, there are a few. Please don't eat or drink in the bedroom, and please wash the dishes before you leave at the end of your stay.

Kanako: I see.

Julie: Oh, and please turn off the lights and the air conditioner when you are not using the room.

Kanako: I will, of course. By the way, what is the latest time I can check out?

Julie: At midday.

Kanako: Got it.

Julie: Do you have any more questions?

Kanako: Yes, just one. Where is the nearest supermarket?

Julie: There's one a few blocks away. Just head in that direction and it's on your left. You can't miss it. It's only a few minutes' walk. They have a great selection of meals that are quick and easy to prepare.

Kanako: Great. I'll check them out. Thanks. The room has a microwave oven and a regular cooker, doesn't it?

Julie: Yes, it does. Well, here's the room, and here are your keys.

Kanako: Thanks a lot.

Julie: Let's go inside, and I'll show you where everything is and how to use the appliances.

1. What kind of accommodation is Kanako staying in?

    (A) A hotel

    (B) A youth hostel

    (C) A dormitory

    (D) A short-stay room for rent

2. What can Kanako do in her accommodation?

    (A) Keep a pet

    (B) Have a party

    (C) Cook meals

    (D) Eat food in the bedroom

3. By what time should Kanako check out?

    (A) 10:00

    (B) 11:00

    (C) 12:00

    (D) 14:00

4. What does Julie give Kanako?

    (A) A map

    (B) The keys to the room

    (C) A form to sign

    (D) Some food

Ⅲ. Fill in the Gaps

As you listen to the conversation again, fill in each gap with the correct word.

Julie: Hi! Are you Kanako? I'm Julie, the 1)_____ of the short-stay room for rent that you booked.

Kanako: Yes, I'm Kanako. Hello, Julie. Pleased to meet you.

Julie: Let me take you to the room. It's not far from here.

Kanako: Thanks.

Julie: Do you have any questions?

Kanako: Err...yes. I read about the room on the website, but I didn't see many 2)_____ mentioned. It said, "No pets" and "No parties." Are there any other rules?

Julie: Yes, there are a few. Please don't eat or drink in the bedroom, and please wash the 3)_____ before you leave at the end of your stay.

Kanako: I see.

Julie: Oh, and please turn off the lights and the air conditioner when you are not using the room.

Kanako: I will, 4)_____ 5)_____. By the way, what is the latest time I can 6)_____ 7)_____?

Julie: At midday.

Kanako: Got it.

Julie: Do you have any more questions?

Kanako: Yes, just one. Where is the nearest supermarket?

Julie: There's one a few blocks away. Just head in that direction and it's on your left. You can't 8)_____ it. It's only a few minutes' walk. They have a great selection of meals that are quick and easy to prepare.

Kanako: Great. I'll check them out. Thanks. The room has a microwave oven and a regular cooker, doesn't it?

Julie: Yes, it does. Well, here's the room, and here are your keys.

Kanako: Thanks a lot.

Julie: Let's go 9)_____, and I'll show you where everything is and how to use the appliances.

IV. Everyday English Phrases

 11

Listen to the audio and write what you hear.

1. ....

2. ....

3. ....

4. ....

V. Incomplete Sentences

Choose the word or phrase in the parentheses that best completes each sentence below.

1. If you are traveling abroad, you will need to (arrange / create) rental accommodation.

2. Finding a place to stay should be (high up / soon after) on your list of priorities.

3. When you are (living in / looking for) a rental flat, you will often see requests for roommates advertised in various places.

4. Sharing a room is often the cheapest way to rent and is also a good way to (make friends / do business).

5. But remember: sharing a room requires patience and (competition / cooperation).

VI. Making Sentences

Unscramble the words in the parentheses to make complete English sentences.

1. すみません、こちらの場所が少しわからなくて到着が遅れました。

   Sorry I'm late, ...

   (a, trouble, had, finding, I, this, little, place)

2. 初めての台湾で、まだ道が不慣れです。

   This is my first time in Taiwan, and ....

   (know, around, I, my, yet, way, don't)

3. 私に出来ることがあれば遠慮なく言って下さい。

   Do not hesitate to ask ....

   (if, I, there, do, is, can, anything)

4. キッチンに冷蔵庫と電子レンジはありますか？

   .... oven in the kitchen?

   (microwave, is, refrigerator, and, a, a, there)

5. 日本にいる間、観光客が知っておく重要な習慣はありますか？

   What local customs .... while
   in Japan?

   (are, know, for, to, a, visitor, important)

Coffee Break

CEFR

皆さん、CEFR って聞いたことがありますか？ CEFR とは外国語（英語に限定しない）の運用能力を同一の基準で測定する国際標準です。能力別に「何ができるか」を示した熟達度があり、下から A1、A2、B1、B2、C1、C2 の 6 段階に分かれています（大学生であれば B1/B2 ぐらいの運用能力はあった方が望ましい）。近年では、文部科学省が、各資格・検定試験（英検、TOEIC、TOEFL、IELTS 等）のスコアと CEFR との対照表を作成し公開しました。しかし、その信頼性については様々な議論があり、これからも引き続き検証が必要な状況です。また、この対照表における各資格・検定試験は、問題、目的（留学であれば TOEFL、IELTS、日本人の実用英語の習得を目的とした英検、ビジネスであれば TOEIC 等）、評価方法等が全く異なるため、それらは比較できません。確かに CEFR は国際標準であり、最近よく耳にしますが、大学生の皆さんは、そこで示される熟達度にとらわれることなく、自身の目的に応じて、各資格・検定試験を選び、目標を定めて、日々の英語学習に励むのが良いのではないでしょうか。

Unit 6

Smartphones and PCs

I. Before You Listen

Match the words on the left with their definitions on the right. If you don't know a word's meaning, take a guess.

1. glad	( )	(A)	to enter; get into
2. setting	( )	(B)	fast
3. connect	( )	(C)	quite; awfully; a little
4. access	( )	(D)	happy; pleased
5. once	( )	(E)	being able to receive messages on the Internet
6. reception	( )	(F)	control position on a phone or computer
7. pretty	( )	(G)	to join the Internet
8. quick	( )	(H)	as soon as

Listen to Kanako's conversation at an Internet cafe and answer the questions that follow.

Kanako: The sign says that free Wi-Fi is available here. I would like to call my family in Japan using LINE. Would you please tell me how to get free Wi-Fi?

Clerk: I'd be glad to. First, go to the connection settings on your smartphone.

Kanako: All right.

Clerk: The network name is "londonabc." Can you see that?

Kanako: I'm sorry. Which one is it?

Clerk: It's "londonabc." Here's the information. Now enter the password. Once you connect successfully, you can get free Internet.

Kanako: Thanks so much. I'd like to send an e-mail from my PC, as well. How do I access the Internet from my PC?

Clerk: It's the same as on your smartphone. Go to the connection settings on your PC, and then enter the information that I just gave you.

Kanako: You mean "londonabc"?

Clerk: Yes, that's right. Just start up your PC, select the network "londonabc," and then enter the same password.

(Kanako tries it.)

Kanako: I've connected.

Clerk: That's great.

Kanako: Uh oh! This connection seems pretty slow. This webpage is taking a long time to open.

Clerk: Then why don't you try moving over there? The reception is usually better by the window.

Kanako: OK. I'll do that.

(Kanako moves near the window.)

Kanako: You were right. It's much quicker over here. Thanks.

1. What does Kanako want to do with her smartphone?
   (A) Download some music
   (B) Watch a movie
   (C) Shop on the Internet
   (D) Talk to her family

2. What does Kanako want to do with her PC?
   (A) Send an e-mail
   (B) Shop on the Internet
   (C) Read the news
   (D) Get it repaired

3. What's the problem with Kanako's internet connection?
   (A) She has forgotten the password.
   (B) It's too expensive.
   (C) She can't find a network to connect to.
   (D) It's too slow.

4. What does Kanako do?
   (A) She moves to another place.
   (B) She turns her computer off and then on again.
   (C) She gives up trying to connect to the Internet.
   (D) She enters a different password.

As you listen to the conversation again, fill in each gap with the correct word.

Kanako: The sign says that free Wi-Fi is ¹⁾_____ here. I would like to call my family in Japan using LINE. Would you please tell me how to get free Wi-Fi?

Clerk: I'd be glad to. First, go to the connection settings on your smartphone.

Kanako: All right.

Clerk: The ²⁾_____ name is "londonabc." Can you see that?

Kanako: I'm sorry. Which one is it?

Clerk: It's "londonabc." Here's the information. Now enter the password. Once you connect successfully, you can get free Internet.

Kanako: Thanks so much. I'd like to send an e-mail from my PC, as well. How do I ³⁾_____ the Internet from my PC?

Clerk: It's the same as on your smartphone. Go to the connection ⁴⁾_____ on your PC, and then ⁵⁾_____ the information that I just gave you.

Kanako: You mean "londonabc"?

Clerk: Yes, that's right. Just start up your PC, select the network "londonabc," and then enter the same password.

(Kanako tries it.)

Kanako: I've connected.

Clerk: That's great.

Kanako: Uh oh! This connection seems pretty slow. This webpage is taking a long time to open.

Clerk: Then why don't you try moving over there? The ⁶⁾_____ is usually better by the window.

Kanako: OK. I'll do that.

(Kanako moves near the window.)

Kanako: You were right. It's much quicker over here. Thanks.

IV. Everyday English Phrases

Listen to the audio and write what you hear.

1. ....

2. ....

3. ....

4. ....

V. Incomplete Sentences

Choose the word that best completes each sentence below.

1. LINE is a piece of software (   ) for calling and instant messaging.

   (A) helped   (B) done   (C) had   (D) designed

2. If you have friends who use the LINE app, you can communicate (   ) them for free via text messages and group chats.

   (A) with   (B) in   (C) on   (D) of

3. LINE includes a VOOM feature that works like the feed (   ) in Facebook and Instagram.

   (A) made   (B) sold   (C) used   (D) charged

4. You need to have the LINE app (   ) on your smartphone to use the PC version of the software.

   (A) created   (B) installed   (C) built   (D) attached

5. To use the software, a QR code will be (   ) on your PC screen.

   (A) displayed   (B) appeared   (C) set   (D) informed

VI. Making Sentences

Unscramble the words in the parentheses to make complete English sentences.

1. 数週間シンガポールを旅しているが、スマホが使えないようだ。

   _____, but I don't seem to be able to use my smartphone here.

   (for, a, visiting, few, I'm, weeks, Singapore)

2. スマホをお持ちですか？よろしければお調べします。

   Do you have your smartphone with you? I _____ like.

   (if, you, for, can, it, you, check)

3. 滞在中に SIM カードを買って、スマホに入れることはできますか？

   Is _____ that I can use in my smartphone while I'm here?

   (to, a, it, buy, SIM, possible, card)

4. SIM を入れ替えてもらえますか？

   Would you _____?

   (for, replacing, card, me, SIM, the, mind)

5. 新しい電話番号はレシートに書いてあります。

   Your _____.

   (your, number, receipt, is, new, on, phone)

Coffee Break

間違えやすい英語表現1

英語で話すとき、間違えやすい表現を集めてみました。文法を理解することが必要ですが、正しい表現を繰り返し声に出してみることで、自然と身につけることができます。

Incorrect: It took for three hours.
Correct: It took three hours.
Incorrect: He went to abroad.
Correct: He went abroad.
Incorrect: I visited to Kyoto.
Correct: I visited Kyoto. I went to Kyoto.
Incorrect: I will go shopping to Tokyu Department Store.
Correct: I will go shopping at Tokyu Department Store.
I will go to Tokyu Department Store to shop.
Awkward: How do you think about that custom?
Natural: What do you think about that custom?
Awkward: I got a friend there.
Natural: I made a friend there.

Unit 7

Using Uber

I. Before You Listen

Match the words on the left with their definitions on the right. If you don't know a word's meaning, take a guess.

1. catch ( )   (A) a drawing or illustration showing rivers, roads, mountains, towns, and other features of an area

2. freelance ( )   (B) the place you are going to

3. symbol ( )   (C) information

4. map ( )   (D) to get on a bus, train, flight, etc.

5. location ( )   (E) sign; icon; logo

6. close ( )   (F) working independently and not as a full-time worker

7. details ( )   (G) near

8. destination ( )   (H) a place or position

II. Listening Practice

Mike and Kanako are walking in the center of London. Listen to their conversation and answer the questions that follow.

Kanako: Hey, Mike. Why don't we catch a taxi to the restaurant?

Mike: Sure. But let's not use a regular taxi. They're too expensive. I have an app on my smartphone that can save us some money.

Kanako: Why's that?

Mike: Well, because it's an app for what is called a ridesharing service. It connects me directly to a freelance driver, not to a taxi company.

Kanako: Interesting. So how does the app work?

Mike: Well, take a look at this map on the app here. That green dot is us. The app knows where we are and shows our location with that green dot.

Kanako: Wow! What are all those car symbols on the map?

Mike: Those show us the nearest drivers. Some of them are very close to us.

Kanako: So how do you call one?

Mike: In this space here, where it says "Where to?", you type in your destination. What was the name of the restaurant again?

Kanako: It's called Sky Steaks.

Mike: OK. Let me just type it in. S-K-Y S-T... Ah, here it is. Now all I have to do is press enter and wait a moment.

Kanako: What was that sound?

Mike: That means there's a driver coming. The app sent a message telling the driver where we are and where we want to go.

Kanako: Gosh! That was so quick and easy! Is that the price? That's cheap!

Mike: I know. It's great, isn't it? You should download the app. It's really convenient.

Kanako: I think I will. By the way, how do you pay?

Mike: I do that through the app, too. It already has my credit-card details.

1. Where are Kanako and Mike going?

    (A) To Mike's home

    (B) To a taxi stand

    (C) To a restaurant

    (D) To a movie

2. How do they get a ride?

    (A) They call a taxi company.

    (B) They request a ride by using a smartphone app.

    (C) They ask a friend to come and get them.

    (D) They wave for a taxi.

3. How does the driver know where Kanako and Mike are going?

    (A) Mike tells the driver.

    (B) Kanako tells the driver.

    (C) Mike types the destination into the app on his smartphone.

    (D) Kanako types the destination into the app on her smartphone.

4. How will they pay for the ride?

    (A) In cash

    (B) By telling the driver their credit-card details

    (C) By check

    (D) By using the app

III. Fill in the Gaps

As you listen to the conversation again, fill in each gap with the correct word.

Kanako: Hey, Mike. Why don't we catch a taxi to the restaurant?

Mike: Sure. But let's not use a regular taxi. They're too expensive. I have an 1) _____ on my smartphone that can 2) _____ us some money.

Kanako: Why's that?

Mike: Well, because it's an app for what is called a ridesharing service. It 3) _____ me directly to a freelance driver, not to a taxi company.

Kanako: Interesting. So how does the app work?

Mike: Well, take a look at this 4) _____ on the app here. That green dot is us. The app knows where we are and shows our location with that green dot.

Kanako: Wow! What are all those car symbols on the map?

Mike: Those show us the nearest drivers. Some of them are very close to us.

Kanako: So how do you call one?

Mike: In this space here, where it says "Where to?", you type in your 5) _____. What was the name of the restaurant again?

Kanako: It's called Sky Steaks.

Mike: OK. Let me just type it in. S-K-Y S-T... Ah, here it is. Now all I have to do is press enter and wait a moment.

Kanako: What was that sound?

Mike: That means there's a driver coming. The app sent a message telling the driver where we are and where we want to go.

Kanako: Gosh! That was so quick and easy! Is that the price? That's cheap!

Mike: I know. It's great, isn't it? You should 6) _____ the app. It's really convenient.

Kanako: I think I will. By the way, how do you 7) _____?

Mike: I do that through the app, too. It already has my credit-card details.

IV. Everyday English Phrases

 15

Listen to the audio and write what you hear.

1. ....

2. ....

3. ....

4. ....

V. Incomplete Sentences

Choose the word from the box that best completes each sentence below.

1. No need to try to hail a taxi from the curb. You can easily request an Uber taxi ride (   ) your smartphone.

2. You'll be automatically charged (   ) the payment method you have selected on your app.

3. Once you confirm that your pick-up and destination addresses are correct, select Uber Taxi (   ) the bottom of your smartphone's screen.

4. When you get (   ) a ride share, the driver already knows where to take you.

5. In Japan, Uber taxis make it a lot easier (   ) non-Japanese speakers to get the rides they need.

(A) at	(B) into	(C) through	(D) on	(E) for
(F) by	(G) beside	(H) under	(I) off	(J) over

VI. Making Sentences

Unscramble the words in the parentheses to make complete English sentences.

1. 脚が疲れました。これ以上、歩きたくありません。

   My legs are tired. _____.

   (any, I, want, more, walk, don't, to)

2. ライドシェアリング用のアプリを使ってみたら？

   Why don't you try to _____?

   (for, an, a, service, use, app, ridesharing)

3. 私は非常に便利なスマホ用のアプリを持っています。

   I _____ my smartphone.

   (convenient, have, on, apps, very)

4. ホテルまでタクシーでいくらですか

   How _____ by taxi?

   (fare, hotel, much, the, the, is, to)

5. 10ポンド50ペンスですか？わかりました。はい、料金です。1ポンドはチップです。

   Ten pounds, fifty? OK. _____ tip.

   (the, a, here's, fare, one-pound, here's, and)

Coffee Break ☕

間違えやすい英語表現2

日本語を英語に直訳するようにして話すと間違えてしまうことがあります。正しい表現を確認し、声に出して言ってみましょう。

Incorrect:	I mistaked.
Correct:	I made a mistake. I was mistaken.
Incorrect:	Let's discuss about the problem.
Correct:	Let's discuss the problem.
	Let's talk about the problem.
Incorrect:	She suggested me to go.
Correct:	She suggested I go.
Incorrect:	He is good personality.
Correct:	He has a good personality.
Incorrect:	Today is tired.
Correct:	I am (got) tired today.
Awkward:	I'm very fine.
Natural:	I'm fine. I'm very well.

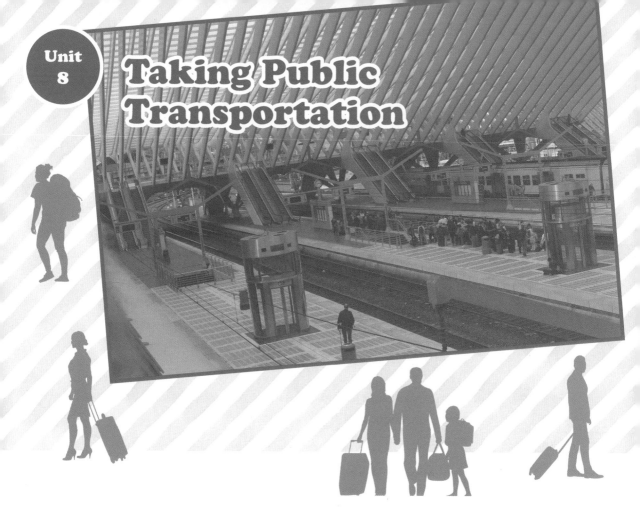

Unit 8
Taking Public Transportation

I. Before You Listen

Match the words or phrases on the left with their definitions on the right. If you don't know a word's or phrase's meaning, take a guess.

1. take ( )   (A) incidentally; also; additionally
2. underground ( )   (B) bargain; method; system
3. on foot ( )   (C) to buy
4. get to ( )   (D) require; need; consume
5. by the way ( )   (E) trip
6. purchase ( )   (F) (by) walking
7. deal ( )   (G) subway
8. journey ( )   (H) arrive

Kanako is going to Wimbledon. She talks to a passerby and then to a station clerk. Listen to her conversations and then answer the questions that follow.

(On the street)

Kanako: Excuse me, can you tell me how to get to the nearest Underground station?

Passerby: Yes, sure. The nearest station is Boston Manor Underground Station, but it'll take you at least 20 minutes on foot.

Kanako: I see. That's quite a long walk. Is there any easier way?

Passerby: Well, yes. Do you want to go into the center of London?

Kanako: No, I want to go to Wimbledon. I have tickets for the tennis tournament.

Passerby: Lucky you! Well, in that case, I think you should take a regular train. It will be quicker.

Kanako: All right. So, where's the nearest regular train station?

Passerby: That's Brentford Station. It's a ten-minute walk from here.

Kanako: Thanks for your help.

Passerby: By the way, the nearest station to the Wimbledon tennis courts is not Wimbledon Station. It's Southfields Underground Station. You'll need to change trains at Wimbledon Station.

Kanako: Oh, thanks for telling me.

(At the station)

Kanako: Excuse me. May I get a ticket for Southfields Underground Station?

Clerk: Yes, certainly. I suggest that you purchase a day Travelcard. You can use it for any buses or trains, and for the Underground. It's a really good deal.

Kanako: OK. Thanks. I'll take one. When's the next train?

Clerk: At 10:35.

Kanako: How long will the journey take?

Clerk: About 30 minutes to Wimbledon Station. After that, you need to change to the District Line on the Underground. It's two stops to Southfields.

1. Why doesn't Kanako go to Boston Manor Underground Station?

    (A) Because it's a long walk.

    (B) Because the Underground is too expensive.

    (C) Because she doesn't know the way there.

    (D) Because the trains have stopped.

2. What is Kanako going to do?

    (A) Go sightseeing

    (B) Watch tennis

    (C) Go shopping

    (D) Watch a show

3. At which station does Kanako buy a Travelcard?

    (A) Boston Manor

    (B) Wimbledon

    (C) Southfields

    (D) Brentford

4. How will Kanako get to her final destination?

    (A) She will go on foot.

    (B) She will take a bus and then an Underground train.

    (C) She will take an Underground train from Brentford Station directly to the tennis tournament.

    (D) She will take a regular train to Wimbledon Station and then change trains to Southfield Station.

III. Fill in the Gaps

As you listen to the conversation again, fill in each gap with the correct word.

(On the street)

Kanako: Excuse me, can you tell me how to get to the [1]_____ Underground station?

Passerby: Yes, sure. The nearest station is Boston Manor Underground Station, but it'll [2]_____ you at least 20 minutes on foot.

Kanako: I see. That's quite a long walk. Is there any easier way?

Passerby: Well, yes. Do you want to go into the [3]_____ of London?

Kanako: No, I want to go to Wimbledon. I have tickets for the tennis tournament.

Passerby: Lucky you! Well, in that case, I think you should take a regular train. It will be quicker.

Kanako: All right. So, where's the nearest regular train station?

Passerby: That's Brentford Station. It's a ten-minute walk from here.

Kanako: Thanks for your help.

Passerby: By the way, the nearest station to the Wimbledon tennis courts is not Wimbledon Station. It's Southfields Underground Station. You'll need to [4]_____ trains at Wimbledon Station.

Kanako: Oh, thanks for telling me.

(At the station)

Kanako: Excuse me. May I get a ticket for Southfields Underground Station?

Clerk: Yes, certainly. I suggest that you purchase a day Travelcard. You can use it for any buses or trains, and for the Underground. It's a really good deal.

Kanako: OK. Thanks. I'll take one. When's the next train?

Clerk: At 10:35.

Kanako: [5]_____ [6]_____ will the journey take?

Clerk: About 30 minutes to Wimbledon Station. After that, you need to change to the District Line on the Underground. It's two [7]_____ to Southfields.

IV. Everyday English Phrases

Listen to the audio and write what you hear.

1. ....

2. ....

3. ....

4. ....

V. Incomplete Sentences

Choose the word or phrase in the parentheses that best completes each sentence below.

1. Various types of public transportation (open up / are available) in New York, including trains, buses, taxis, airplanes and ships.

2. You can (pick up / catch) a free timetable of local services at each station.

3. Subway stations (belong to / are connected to) ground level through underground passageways.

4. Prepaid cards allow you to (find / go through) an automatic ticket gate simply by touching the card on the reader.

5. In addition to general buses and sightseeing bus services, some local buses (are operated / are appointed) free of charge.

VI. Making Sentences

Unscramble the words in the parentheses to make complete English sentences.

1. 徒歩で少なくとも 10 分かかります。

   _____ on foot.

   (ten, least, take, you, at, minutes, it'll)

2. タイムズ・スクエア駅に行く電車はこれでいいですか？

   _____ Times Square Station?

   (this, bound, train, is, the, for, right)

3. 往復切符を買っていたらもっと安かったでしょうか？

   Would it have been _____ ticket?

   (had, a, if, cheaper, we, round-trip, bought)

4. 私は歩いて行きましたが、バスに乗ればよかったです。

   I went on foot, _____ .

   (by, could, I, gone, bus, have, but)

5. 私は電車に切符を落としてしまいました。どうすればよいでしょうか？

   _____ the train. What should I do?

   (on, ticket, have, dropped, I, must, my)

Coffee Break

間違えやすい英語表現3

「こんな時にはこう表現する」と理解して慣れておくとスマートに伝わる表現があります。正しい表現を確認しながら、何度も声に出して言ってみましょう。

Incorrect:	It is a twenty-minutes walk.
Correct:	It is a twenty-minute walk.
Incorrect:	I and my friend took a trip.
Correct:	My friend and I took a trip.
Incorrect:	I went there on last Friday.
Correct:	I went there on Friday. I went there last Friday.
Incorrect:	I very enjoyed it. I very liked it.
Correct:	I liked (enjoyed) it very much.
Incorrect:	She is kind for me.
Correct:	She is kind to me.
Awkward:	I like to sing a song, paint a picture, and read a book.
Natural:	I like to sing, to paint, and to read.

Unit 9 · A Study Tour

I. Before You Listen

Match the words on the left with their definitions on the right. If you don't know a word's meaning, take a guess.

1. organize   ( )   (A) animals living in nature
2. cover   ( )   (B) a plan or list of the places you will visit on a trip
3. admission   ( )   (C) a display in a museum or gallery
4. itinerary   ( )   (D) to make arrangements for an activity; arrange; get ready
5. provide   ( )   (E) natural surroundings; nature
6. exhibition   ( )   (F) to be or have enough money to pay for something
7. environment   ( )   (G) the cost of entrance to a concert, sports events, etc.
8. wildlife   ( )   (H) to make available; supply; give; furnish

II. Listening Practice

Listen to the conversation below between a student and a teacher and then answer the questions that follow.

Professor: Yes, come in! Oh, hello, Peter. How can I help you?

Peter: Excuse me, Professor, but I'd like to ask you a few questions about the university study tour. I heard that you are organizing the tour. Is that right?

Professor: Yes, I am. What would you like to know, Peter?

Peter: How many days will the tour last?

Professor: It's a three-day trip.

Peter: How much does it cost?

Professor: The price is 230 pounds.

Peter: Will that cover everything?

Professor: Not quite. It will cover your train trip to London, your Travelcard for traveling around London, and your hotel expenses. It will also cover any admission or event fees.

Peter: What about food?

Professor: Your breakfast and evening meal will be provided at the hotel. You will need to pay for lunch, though.

Peter: I see. Can you tell me about the itinerary?

Professor: Well, on the first day, we'll travel to London. We should arrive at the hotel by midday. We'll check in and then take the underground to the Science Museum. The museum has two excellent exhibitions about the environment.

Peter: That sounds really interesting.

Professor: On the second day, in the morning, we will go to the Thames Barrier and take a guided tour. We'll learn all about the history of the River Thames and about the river's environment and wildlife. In the afternoon, we'll visit the British Museum.

Peter: My friend Kanako from Japan wants to take the tour, too.

Professor: Great! I'm sure you'll both enjoy yourselves and learn a lot.

1. How long is the study tour?
   (A) Two days
   (B) Three days
   (C) Four days
   (D) One week

2. What's the price of the trip?
   (A) It's free.
   (B) 120 pounds
   (C) 230 pounds
   (D) 320 pounds

3. Where will the students go for the study tour?
   (A) Bristol
   (B) Manchester
   (C) London
   (D) Newcastle

4. What will the students need to pay extra for?
   (A) The museum admission fee
   (B) The river boat ride
   (C) Their lunches
   (D) Traveling around London

5. What will happen on day 1?
   (A) The students will see some exhibitions in a museum.
   (B) The students will attend a lecture on the environment.
   (C) The students will go on a guided tour of the Thames.
   (D) The students will watch an educational video on wildlife.

Ⅲ. Fill in the Gaps

As you listen to the conversation again, fill in each gap with the correct word.

Professor: Yes, come in! Oh, hello, Peter. How can I help you?

Peter: Excuse me, Professor, but I'd like to ask you a few questions about the university study tour. I heard that you are ¹⁾_____ the tour. Is that right?

Professor: Yes, I am. What would you like to know, Peter?

Peter: ²⁾_____ ³⁾_____ days will the tour last?

Professor: It's a three-day trip.

Peter: How much does it cost?

Professor: The price is 230 pounds.

Peter: Will that ⁴⁾_____ everything?

Professor: Not quite. It will cover your train trip to London, your Travelcard for traveling around London, and your hotel ⁵⁾_____. It will also cover any admission or event ⁶⁾_____.

Peter: What about food?

Professor: Your breakfast and evening meal will be provided at the hotel. You will need to pay for lunch, though.

Peter: I see. Can you tell me about the itinerary?

Professor: Well, on the first day, we'll travel to London. We should ⁷⁾_____ at the hotel by midday. We'll check in and then take the underground to the Science Museum. The museum has two excellent exhibitions about the ⁸⁾_____.

Peter: That sounds really interesting.

Professor: On the second day, in the morning, we will go to the Thames Barrier and take a ⁹⁾_____ ¹⁰⁾_____. We'll learn all about the history of the River Thames and about the river's environment and wildlife. In the afternoon, we'll visit the British Museum.

Peter: My friend Kanako from Japan wants to take the tour, too.

Professor: Great! I'm sure you'll both enjoy yourselves and learn a lot.

Ⅳ. Everyday English Phrases

Listen to the audio and write what you hear.

1. ....

2. ....

3. ....

4. ....

Ⅴ. Incomplete Sentences

Choose the word that best completes each sentence below.

1. Learn about environmental sustainability (   ) working on a certified organic farm.

   (A) by　　　(B) with　　　(C) for　　　　(D) on

2. Join us for a (   ) tour of our farm, which is world famous for its advanced farming methods.

   (A) guide　　(B) guiding　　(C) guidance　　(D) guided

3. Our activities are linked (   ) such important global issues as biodiversity and sustainable agriculture.

   (A) of　　　(B) to　　　　(C) at　　　　(D) for

4. If your group is from a university or college, our Academic Tour program would be happy to (   ) a tour that fits your needs.

   (A) start　　(B) teach　　(C) arrange　　(D) show

5. You will be paired (   ) with some local students, take classes and participate in exciting activities together.

   (A) in　　　(B) on　　　(C) to　　　　(D) up

VI. Making Sentences

Unscramble the words in the parentheses to make complete English sentences.

1. 明日のスタディツアーに登録したいのですが。

   I'd _____ tour.

   (sign, for, study, up, like, tomorrow's, to)

2. ツアー料金には食事代と入館料が含まれています。

   The tour cost _____ .

   (and, meals, any, fees, covers, any, admission)

3. 最終的な人数が何名になるか分かりませんが、今のところ 4 名の学生は確実です。

   I'm not sure what the final number will be, _____ .

   (but, have, students, four, so, confirmed, far)

4. ロンドン東部のザ・クリスタルは世界で最も環境にやさしい建物の 1 つです。

   The Crystal in the eastern part of London is _____ .

   (most, of, the, buildings, one, eco-friendly, world's)

5. こんなに素敵な田園風景をこれまで見たことはありません。

   Never before _____ .

   (I, countryside, such, have, scenery, beautiful, seen)

Coffee Break

間違えやすい英語表現4

時制にまつわる表現は日本人には難しく感じることがあります。繰り返し言ってみることで、正しい表現に慣れましょう。

Incorrect: I don't decide yet.
Correct: I haven't decided yet.
Incorrect: Do you make a plan for the weekend?
Correct: Have you made any plans for the weekend?
Incorrect: I had a good memory of it.
Correct: I have a good memory of it.
Incorrect: It costed fifty dollars.
Correct: It cost fifty dollars. (=It was fifty dollars.)
Incorrect: I went there two years before. I will go there two years after.
Correct: I went there two years ago. I will go there two years from now.
Awkward: Recently I am busy.
Natural: Recently I have been busy.

Unit 10 Music Festivals

I. Before You Listen

Match the words on the left with their definitions on the right. If you don't know a word's meaning, take a guess.

1. headline ( )   (A) different; all kinds of
2. hold ( )   (B) amazing; incredible; fascinating
3. facilities ( )   (C) the amount of space between two things
4. various ( )   (D) to play on radio or show on TV
5. awesome ( )   (E) the main performer or act in a show or concert
6. broadcast ( )   (F) condition
7. state ( )   (G) equipment or place used for a particular purpose
8. distance ( )   (H) to produce; put on; stage

Kanako is talking to Mike about a famous UK music festival. Listen to the conversation and then answer the questions that follow.

Kanako: How about going to a music festival? I'd like to go to one while I'm here, if possible.

Mike: Well, there are a few. They usually take place in the summer. The biggest one I know of is the Glastonbury Festival. The headline bands there are often some of the most famous bands in the world.

Kanako: Is Glastonbury in London?

Mike: No it isn't. Glastonbury is the name of a small town in the county of Somerset. The Glastonbury Festival takes place on a farm near the town.

Kanako: On a farm? Is it a one-day event?

Mike: No. It lasts for five days.

Kanako: Awesome! So where do people sleep?

Mike: They camp out in tents in nearby fields. The festival organizers provide various campsite facilities like toilets and showers. I hear, though, that by the last day of the festival, the toilets are usually in a terrible state.

Kanako: That doesn't sound very nice.

Mike: No, it isn't. But that doesn't stop people from going there. Last year, around two-hundred thousand people attended the festival.

Kanako: Wow! That's a lot! So, where exactly is Glastonbury?

Mike: It's in the South West of England.

Kanako: How far away from London is that?

Mike: Well, it takes between three and four hours by train.

Kanako: Oh, that's quite a distance. I don't think I'll be going there, then.

Mike: You couldn't go anyway. They say the tickets are already sold out this year. They always go very quickly. You can watch the festival on TV, though. It's usually broadcast live.

1. How long does the festival last?
    (A) One day
    (B) Three days
    (C) Five days
    (D) One week

2. Where do people who attend the festival usually sleep?
    (A) In nearby hotels
    (B) In tents
    (C) In farm buildings
    (D) In people's houses

3. How many people went to the festival last year?
    (A) Around 2,000
    (B) Around 20,000
    (C) Around 200,000
    (D) Around 2,000,000

4. Where is Glastonbury?
    (A) It's in London.
    (B) It's near London.
    (C) It's in the Southwest of England.
    (D) It's in the Southeast of England.

5. Why won't Kanako be able to go to the festival this year?
    (A) It's too expensive.
    (B) The tickets are sold out.
    (C) She is ill.
    (D) The festival has already been held.

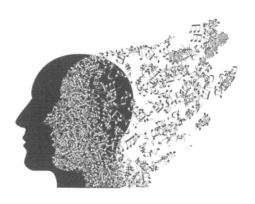

As you listen to the conversation again, fill in each gap with the correct word.

Kanako: How about going to a music [1)]_____? I'd like to go to one while I'm here, if possible.

Mike: Well, there are a few. They usually take place in the summer. The biggest one I know of is the Glastonbury Festival. The [2)]_____ bands there are often some of the most [3)]_____ bands in the world.

Kanako: Is Glastonbury in London?

Mike: No it isn't. Glastonbury is the name of a small [4)]_____ in the county of Somerset. The Glastonbury Festival takes place on a [5)]_____ near the town.

Kanako: On a farm? Is it a one-day [6)]_____?

Mike: No. It [7)]_____ for five days.

Kanako: Awesome! So where do people sleep?

Mike: They camp out in tents in nearby [8)]_____. The festival organizers provide various campsite facilities like toilets and showers. I hear, though, that by the last day of the festival, the toilets are usually in a terrible state.

Kanako: That doesn't sound very nice.

Mike: No, it isn't. But that doesn't stop people from going there. Last year, around two-hundred thousand people [9)]_____ the festival.

Kanako: Wow! That's a lot! So, where exactly is Glastonbury?

Mike: It's in the South West of England.

Kanako: How far away from London is that?

Mike: Well, it takes between three and four hours by train.

Kanako: Oh, that's quite a distance. I don't think I'll be going there, then.

Mike: You couldn't go anyway. They say the tickets are already [10)]_____ [11)]_____ this year. They always go very quickly. You can watch the festival on TV, though. It's usually [12)]_____ live.

Ⅳ. Everyday English Phrases

 21

Listen to the audio and write what you hear.

1. ....

2. ....

3. ....

4. ....

Ⅴ. Incomplete Sentences

Choose the word from the box that best completes each sentence below.

1. (　　) the Tanglewood 2020 Online Festival closing soon, we want to thank you for being part of our Tanglewood family.

2. The COVID-19 pandemic has reduced the number of customers coming (　　) the door of the music shop.

3. The music festival is an opportunity for music lovers to get involved (　　) an eco-friendly activity.

4. The organization, which focuses its efforts (　　) ending global poverty, has announced plans to stage a massive music festival.

5. To make the concert possible, the organizer teamed (　　) with a consultancy firm.

(A) on	(B) along	(C) by	(D) with	(E) up
(F) in	(G) for	(H) through	(I) of	(J) to

VI. Making Sentences

Unscramble the words in the parentheses to make complete English sentences.

1. ライブ音楽に行ってみたいな。どこかお薦めはありますか？

   I want to go and see some live music. Is _____ ?

   (you, that, anywhere, recommend, there)

2. ボストンには音楽の催し会場が多いです。

   There _____ .

   (venues, of, are, in, lots, music, Boston)

3. 聖歌隊のリサイタルはここで開かれるんですか？

   Is _____ recital?

   (choir, the, place, for, this, the, right)

4. 今日のコンサートに行けなかったなんて残念でしたね。明日のコンサートのチケットを手に入れるのは難しいかもしれません。

   I'm sorry you missed today's concert. You _____
   for tomorrow's concert.

   (getting, time, may, difficult, tickets, a, have)

5. 「チケットは持っていますよ」「それはよかった。あなたは忘れたんじゃないかと思っていました」

   "I have our tickets." "That's good. I _____ ."

   (had, afraid, them, you, that, forgotten, was)

Coffee Break

間違えやすい英語表現 5

旅行に行ったときは、家族や友人に絵はがきや写真を添えたメールなどで旅の様子を伝えられるといいですね。きっと喜ばれることでしょう。よくある間違いを集めてみましたので、正しい表現を確認しましょう。

Incorrect:	I went sightseeing to Nikko.
Correct:	I went sightseeing in Nikko.
Incorrect:	It is an historic place.
Correct:	It is an historical place.
Incorrect:	This photo is of Izu which I went on my vacation.
Correct:	This photo is of Izu where I went on my vacation.
Incorrect:	It is so beautiful place.
Correct:	It is so beautiful. It is such a beautiful place.
Awkward:	I hope you will give me an email soon.
Natural:	I hope you will send me an email soon.
Awkward:	Please send my regards to your family.
Natural:	Please give my regards to your family.

Unit 11 — Food

I. Before You Listen

Match the words and phrases on the left with their definitions on the right. If you don't know a word's meaning, take a guess.

1. care for ( )
2. main ( )
3. portion ( )
4. texture ( )
5. starter ( )
6. sour ( )
7. appetite ( )
8. go well with ( )

(A) a small dish served as the first part of a meal; appetizer

(B) the way that a food feels in your mouth (soft, hard, chewy, etc.)

(C) having a taste like a lemon or vinegar

(D) to taste good with; be a good combination

(E) a desire for food; hunger; need to eat

(F) most important; largest

(G) to like; enjoy; be fond of

(H) an amount of food for one person

II. Listening Practice

Kanako and Mike are talking about food. Listen to their conversation and then answer the questions that follow.

Kanako: Mike, there's a drink here that the menu says is fizzy. I don't understand what "fizzy" means.

Mike: It means that the drink has bubbles in it. Like cola or lemonade.

Kanako: I see. Er...I don't like the sound of that. I think I'll just have water. Oh, and there's a fiery Thai curry here in the main-dish section. What does "fiery" mean?

Mike: It means that the dish is really spicy. You know...hot. There are probably a lot of chili peppers in it.

Kanako: That sounds interesting, but I don't really feel like having something spicy right now. What are you going to get as your main dish?

Mike: I think I'll go for the breaded fish and chips.

Kanako: Breaded fish? What does that mean? Is it fish served with a slice of bread?

Mike: No. It means that the fish is covered in breadcrumbs and deep-fried in hot oil. It's got a really nice crunchy texture. And chips are fried potatoes.

Kanako: That sounds good, but I think I'd like something a bit healthier. There's a gazpacho soup here. Do you know what that is?

Mike: It's a cold soup made with tomatoes, so it sometimes tastes a bit sour.

Kanako: That sounds interesting. I think I'll try that.

Mike: That's a starter, so it won't be very big. Do you want to order another dish as well?

Kanako: Portions in England are a bit bigger than they are in Japan. So there might be too much food for me.

Mike: How about we share another dish then? Don't worry. I have a big appetite. If you can't finish it, I'm sure I can.

Kanako: OK.

Mike: There's a bagel here with avocado, salmon, and cream cheese that sounds really tasty.

Kanako: Good idea. Let's share a bagel. It'll go well with my soup. Shall I call the waiter?

1. Where are Kanako and Mike?
   (A) In Mike's kitchen
   (B) In Kanako's rental room
   (C) At a restaurant
   (D) In a supermarket deli

2. What does Kanako choose to drink?
   (A) Cola
   (B) Lemonade
   (C) Wine
   (D) Water

3. What does "fiery" mean?
   (A) Spicy
   (B) Chewy
   (C) Crunchy
   (D) Sour

4. What is Mike's main dish?
   (A) A bagel
   (B) Fish and Chips
   (C) Thai Curry
   (D) Gazpacho Soup

5. What dish are Mike and Kanako going to share?
   (A) A bagel
   (B) Fish and Chips
   (C) Thai Curry
   (D) Gazpacho Soup

Ⅲ. Fill in the Gaps

As you listen to the conversation again, fill in each gap with the correct word.

Kanako: Mike, there's a drink here that the ¹⁾_____ says is fizzy. I don't understand what "fizzy" means.

Mike: It means that the drink has bubbles in it. Like cola or lemonade.

Kanako: I see. Er...I don't like the sound of that. I think I'll just have water. Oh, and there's a fiery Thai curry here in the main-dish section. What does "fiery" mean?

Mike: It means that the dish is really ²⁾_____. You know...hot. There are probably a lot of chili peppers in it.

Kanako: That sounds interesting, but I don't really ³⁾_____ ⁴⁾_____ having something spicy right now. What are you going to get as your ⁵⁾_____ ⁶⁾_____?

Mike: I'll think I'll go for the breaded fish and chips.

Kanako: Breaded fish? What does that mean? Is it fish served with a slice of bread?

Mike: No. It means that the fish is covered in breadcrumbs and deep-fried in hot oil. It's got a really nice ⁷⁾_____ texture. And chips are fried potatoes.

Kanako: That sounds good, but I think I'd like something a bit healthier. There's a gazpacho soup here. Do you know what that is?

Mike: It's a cold soup made with tomatoes, so it sometimes ⁸⁾_____ a bit sour.

Kanako: That sounds interesting. I think I'll try that.

Mike: That's a ⁹⁾_____, so it won't be very big. Do you want to order another dish as well?

Kanako: ¹⁰⁾_____ in England are a bit bigger than they are in Japan. So there might be too much food for me.

Mike: How about we share another dish then? Don't worry. I have a big ¹¹⁾_____. If you can't finish it, I'm sure I can.

Kanako: OK.

Mike: There's a bagel here with avocado, salmon, and cream cheese that sounds really tasty.

Kanako: Good idea. Let's share a bagel. It'll go well with my soup. Shall I call the ¹²⁾_____?

IV. Everyday English Phrases

 23

Listen to the audio and write what you hear.

1. ....

2. ....

3. ....

4. ....

V. Incomplete Sentences

Choose the word in the parentheses that best completes each sentence below.

1. The classic combination of breaded fish and fried potatoes that is now popular around the world originated (on / in) England.

2. Foreign spices have had a huge impact (on / into) English cuisine.

3. The dish is packed (with / on) heart-healthy fats called omega-3 fatty acids.

4. By doing everything with my own two hands, I transmit my love and devotion (for / to) the food.

5. Over the past year, a new wave of ethnic food options has popped (up / off) in Tokyo.

VI. Making Sentences

Unscramble the words in the parentheses to make complete English sentences.

1. あの人が食べている同じ料理を下さい。メニューのどこにありますか?

   May _____ person is having?

   Where's that on the menu?

   (have, as, same, I, the, that, dish)

2. このソーセージは savory と書いてありますが、どんな意味ですか?

   _____. What does "savory" mean?

   (says, that, savory, are, it, sausages, the)

3. 卵の入った料理は食べられません。卵アレルギーなんです。

   _____. I'm allergic to eggs.

   (avoid, eggs, have, I, containing, to, foods)

4. ランチにフィッシュ・アンド・チップスはいかがですか?

   Why _____ lunch?

   (the, try, and, fish, for, not, chips)

5. これまで食べた中で、これは一番おいしい食べ物です。

   This _____.

   (I've, best, the, food, ever, is, tasted)

Coffee Break

間違えやすい英語表現6

「旅行する」という表現について、以下の文章の中に trip、travel を入れてみましょう。必要な場合は、その形を変えて下さい。

1. I took a _____ last month. I like _____ very much. I _____ whether I can. I am saving money for my next _____ now.

2. He takes many business _____. He often _____ in Europe and America. He is on a _____ right now.

3. I _____ in Europe last summer. The _____ through the Swiss Alps was spectacular. I often think about that _____ now.

4. We can learn about many things through _____. We can meet other people who are _____ too. A _____ is a valuable experience.

Answers: 1. trip, traveling, travel, trip   2. trips, travels, trip
               3. traveled, trip, trip   4. traveling, traveling, trip

Shopping

I. Before You Listen

Match the words and phrases on the left with their definitions on the right. If you don't know a word's or phrase's meaning, take a guess.

1. actually ( )   (A) a decorative design on a piece of clothing
2. browse ( )   (B) of course; sure
3. plain ( )   (C) as a matter of fact; in fact
4. pattern ( )   (D) a place to try on clothes
5. rack ( )   (E) I'm sorry, but…
6. fitting room ( )   (F) without decoration; simple
7. certainly ( )   (G) a frame or shelf, usually with bars or hooks for hanging things on
8. I'm afraid… ( )   (H) to look around at the goods for sale in a shop

II. Listening Practice

Kanako is out shopping in a clothing store and talks to a sales assistant. Listen to the conversations and answer the questions that follow.

Assistant: Hello. May I help you?

Kanako: No, thanks. I'm just browsing.

Assistant: Well, let me know if you need my help. Take your time.

Kanako: Will do, thanks... Actually, do you have this T-shirt in any different colors?

Assistant: Yes, we do. The plain ones come in red, pink, purple, and blue. We also have them in different patterns. Those are on this rack here.

Kanako: Oh, I see. I like this flower pattern. May I try it on?

Assistant: Yes, certainly. The fitting rooms are over there.

Kanako: OK, thanks.

(Later)

Assistant: How was it?

Kanako: I like it. Fits perfectly. I'll take it.

Assistant: Great! By the way, we have a "Buy 2 Get 1 Free" deal on this week.

Kanako: I'm afraid I don't know what that means.

Assistant: Well, if you buy two of these T-shirts, we'll give you another one free.

Kanako: In that case, I'll take two plain ones as well. The pink one and the blue one.

Assistant: All right. Would you like anything else?

Kanako: No, thanks. I'll just take these.

Assistant: Let's go to the cash register, then. How would you like to pay, cash or credit card?

Kanako: Credit card, please. Here's my card.

Assistant: Thanks. The total is 50 pounds.

1. Why does Kanako say "Actually"?
   - (A) She has decided to buy something.
   - (B) She isn't really "just browsing."
   - (C) She doesn't understand the assistant.
   - (D) She doesn't know what "Take your time" means.

2. What does Kanako buy?
   - (A) Clothes
   - (B) Books
   - (C) Make-up
   - (D) Food

3. How many items does Kanako purchase?
   - (A) One
   - (B) Two
   - (C) Three
   - (D) Four

4. Why was Kanako's total less than the usual cost?
   - (A) She got one item for free.
   - (B) She got a 10% discount.
   - (C) She bought second-hand clothing.
   - (D) Everything was half-price.

5. How does Kanako pay?
   - (A) In cash
   - (B) By credit card
   - (C) Using her debit card
   - (D) On her smartphone app

As you listen to the conversation again, fill in each gap with the correct word.

Assistant: Hello. May I help you?

Kanako: No, thanks. I'm just 1)_____.

Assistant: Well, let me know if you need my help. Take your time.

Kanako: Will do, thanks... Actually, do you have this T-shirt in any different colors?

Assistant: Yes, we do. The 2)_____ ones come in red, pink, purple, and blue. We also have them in different patterns. Those are on this rack here.

Kanako: Oh, I see. I like this flower pattern. May I 3)_____ 4)_____ 5)_____ ?

Assistant: Yes, certainly. The 6)_____ 7)_____ are over there.

Kanako: OK, thanks.

(Later)

Assistant: How was it?

Kanako: I like it. Fits perfectly. I'll take it.

Assistant: Great! By the way, we have a "Buy 2 Get 1 Free" deal on this week.

Kanako: I'm afraid I don't know what that means.

Assistant: Well, if you buy two of these T-shirts, we'll give you another one free.

Kanako: In that case, I'll take two plain ones as well. The pink one and the blue one.

Assistant: All right. Would you like anything 8)_____?

Kanako: No, thanks. I'll just take these.

Assistant: Let's go to the cash 9)_____, then. How would you like to pay, cash or credit card?

Kanako: Credit card, please. Here's my card.

Assistant: Thanks. The 10)_____ is 50 pounds.

IV. Everyday English Phrases

 25

Listen to the audio and write down the sentences or phrases that you hear.

1. ....

2. ....

3. ....

4. ....

V. Incomplete Sentences

Choose the phrase that best completes each sentence below.

1. All our electrical and mechanical items (   ) a guarantee.

   (A) guard against   (B) come with   (C) keep up   (D) are reserved for

2. Excuse me. I bought these shoes a week ago and the sole is already (   ).

   (A) showing up   (B) cutting down   (C) separating from   (D) coming off

3. Recycle shops are (   ) popularity these days.

   (A) growing in   (B) accounting for (C) dealing with   (D) adding to

4. The COVID-19 pandemic (   ) many shops of all kinds to shut down.

   (A) has spread   (B) has helped   (C) has forced   (D) has resulted

5. How many colors does this jacket (   )?

   (A) come in   (B) take out   (C) carry over   (D) come with

VI. Making Sentences

Unscramble the words in the parentheses to make complete English sentences.

1. 家族へのおみやげを探しています。

   I'm _____ .

   (family, for, souvenirs, my, some, looking, for)

2. これは私には少し大きすぎます。小さいサイズはありますか？

   This _____ . Do you have a smaller size?

   (large, me, little, for, a, is, too)

3. きれいなテーブルクロスですが、家のテーブルには長さが足りません。

   That's a beautiful table cloth, but it's _____ .

   (nearly, table, enough, for, our, long, not)

4. あの古本は5万ドルもの高値で売れました。

   That _____ fifty-thousand dollars.

   (as, as, old, for, much, sold, book)

5. プレゼント用に包んでもらえますか？

   _____ ?

   (you, it, a, as, can, gift, wrap)

Sports Events

I. Before You Listen

Match the words and phrases on the left with their definitions on the right. If you don't know a word's or phrase's meaning, take a guess.

1. court	( )	(A)	a player or team that is expected to win
2. match	( )	(B)	the grounds and buildings of a college or other school
3. favorite	( )	(C)	right now; these days; recently
4. My pleasure.	( )	(D)	to want to know (about) something; feel curious about
5. wonder	( )	(E)	an area specially made for playing sports or games like basketball or tennis
6. campus	( )	(F)	extra; kept in reserve for possible use later
7. at the moment	( )	(G)	a sports contest between two teams or players
8. spare	( )	(H)	You're welcome; No problem; I'm happy to do it.

II. Listening Practice

Kanako is talking to Mike. Listen to their conversation and then answer the questions that follow.

Kanako: Hi, Mike. Thanks for getting me these tickets to the tennis tournament.

Mike: My pleasure. These tickets are good for all the courts, so we can watch lots of different matches today. Is there a match you'd especially like to watch?

Kanako: Well, the Japanese player Kei Nishikori is playing on Court 1 soon. I'd love to see his match.

Mike: Then let's go and watch that. It should be a good match. He is one of the favorites to win the tournament.

Kanako: I know. He's playing really well at the moment. He's ranked number 3 in the world. No Japanese male player has ever got that high before.

Mike: He's definitely a great player. By the way, Kanako, I was wondering: Do you play tennis yourself?

Kanako: Yes, I do.

Mike: How often do you play?

Kanako: I usually play twice a week when I'm home in Japan.

Mike: Where do you play?

Kanako: At my university campus. It has several courts. Actually, I'm on our university's tennis team.

Mike: Gosh! You must be very good!

Kanako: Not really. But when I was a child, I had lessons, so I can play a bit. I really enjoy it.

Mike: Did you know that I play tennis, too?

Kanako: No. I had no idea.

Mike: We should play sometime soon before you go back to Japan. You could come and play at my local tennis club.

Kanako: That would be fantastic. But I'm afraid I left my tennis racket in Japan. I didn't think I'd get a chance to play here.

Mike: Don't worry. I have a spare racket that you can borrow.

1. Where are Kanako and Mike?
   (A) At a tennis tournament
   (B) On a tennis court
   (C) Watching tennis on TV
   (D) At a sports supply shop

2. What will Mike and Kanako do next?
   (A) Watch a tennis match
   (B) Play a game of tennis
   (C) Buy tickets for the tennis tournament
   (D) Have lunch

3. Which of these is NOT true or NOT inferred about Kei Nishikori?
   (A) He is expected to win the tournament.
   (B) He is ranked the number 3 in the world.
   (C) He is the first Japanese player to play in this tournament.
   (D) He is ranked higher than any previous Japanese player.

4. How often does Kanako usually play tennis when she is home in Japan?
   (A) Once a week
   (B) Twice a week
   (C) Three times a week
   (D) Four times a week

5. What do Mike and Kanako plan to do someday?
   (A) Play tennis together
   (B) Buy a tennis racket for Kanako
   (C) Take some tennis lessons
   (D) Meet and talk to Kei Nishikori

As you listen to the conversation again, fill in each gap with the correct word.

Kanako: Hi, Mike. Thanks for getting me these tickets to the tennis tournament.

Mike: My pleasure. These tickets are good for all the courts, so we can watch lots of different ¹⁾_____ today. Is there a match you'd ²⁾_____ like to watch?

Kanako: Well, the Japanese player Kei Nishikori is playing on Court 1 soon. I'd love to see his match.

Mike: Then let's go and watch that. It should be a good match. He is one of the favorites to ³⁾_____ the ⁴⁾_____.

Kanako: I know. He's playing really well at the moment. He's ⁵⁾_____ number 3 in the world. No Japanese male player has ever got that high before.

Mike: He's definitely a great player. By the way, Kanako, I was wondering: Do you play tennis ⁶⁾_____?

Kanako: Yes, I do.

Mike: How ⁷⁾_____ do you play?

Kanako: I usually play twice a week when I'm home in Japan.

Mike: Where do you play?

Kanako: At my university ⁸⁾_____. It has several courts. Actually, I'm on our university's tennis team.

Mike: Gosh! You must be very good!

Kanako: Not really. But when I was a child, I had lessons, so I can play a ⁹⁾_____. I really enjoy it.

Mike: Did you know that I play tennis, too?

Kanako: No. I had no idea.

Mike: We should play sometime soon before you go back to Japan. You could come and play at my ¹⁰⁾_____ tennis club.

Kanako: That would be fantastic. But I'm afraid I left my tennis racket in Japan. I didn't think I'd get a chance to play here.

Mike: Don't worry. I have a ¹¹⁾_____ racket that you can ¹²⁾_____.

Ⅳ. Everyday English Phrases

Listen to the audio and write down the sentences or phrases that you hear.

1. ....

2. ....

3. ....

4. ....

V. Incomplete Sentences

Choose the word from the box that best completes each sentence below. (Use each word only once.)

1. Thousands of tennis fans descend (   ) Wimbledon in Southwest London every summer.

2. In soccer, the role (   ) the forward, also known as the attacker, is to score goals.

3. When soccer players do something bad, they are given a red card and sent (   ) the field.

4. Ichiro retired (   ) professional baseball after getting a combined 4,367 hits in Japan and the US.

5. In baseball, the closer is the pitcher who comes (   ) of the bullpen to try to save his team's win.

(A) over	(B) for	(C) out	(D) of	(E) beyond
(F) from	(G) on	(H) off	(I) to	(J) with

Ⅵ. Making Sentences

Unscramble the words in the parentheses to make complete English sentences.

1. 「試合はいつ始まりますか？」「まさにいま、スケジュール通りに始まるところです」

   "When is the game supposed to start?" "It ...."

   (now, start, is, to, scheduled, about)

2. ワールドカップの決勝の結果についてどう思いましたか？

   .... of the World Cup final?

   (you, think, result, did, what, of, the)

3. 控えの選手は全力で試合をして、ボールさばきも良かったです。

   The substitute brought a lot of energy into the game ....

   (and, the, care, good, took, of, ball)

4. 子どもの頃からテニスのレッスンを受けていました。いま大学のチームでプレーを楽しんでいます。

   I had .... Now I enjoy playing for

   my university team.

   (when, tennis, I, a, lessons, was, child)

5. 次の試合は必ずそこに行きたいな。

   I'm sure ...., then.

   (game, there, be, next, the, for, I'll)

Unit 14 Amusement

I. Before You Listen

Match the words on the left with their definitions on the right. If you don't know a word's meaning, take a guess.

1. amusement ( ) (A) very wet

2. attractions ( ) (B) describing something that protects against water

3. altogether ( ) (C) type; kind

4. soaked ( ) (D) spattered water or other liquid

5. queue ( ) (E) interesting or enjoyable things to see and do at an amusement park

6. waterproof ( ) (F) a leisure activity; an enjoyable way to spend one's time

7. splash ( ) (G) in all; in total

8. sort ( ) (H) a line of people waiting to see, buy, or do something

Kanako is talking to Mike. Listen to their conversation and then answer the questions that follow.

Mike: This is the largest amusement park in the UK, Kanako. Let's look at the map and see where all the best attractions are.

Kanako: Wow! This park has so much to see and do! How many roller-coaster rides are there?

Mike: I think there are five altogether.

Kanako: That many? I want to try them all!

Mike: Me, too. But I don't think we have time to do them all today! The roller-coaster rides are really popular and, because it's the weekend, it's really busy today. We're here for two days. We could do the less popular rides today and then do the more popular rides tomorrow. Tomorrow is Monday, so it won't be so crowded.

Kanako: That sounds like a good idea. Hey, Mike. What's that ride over there? It looks really fun.

Mike: Some sort of river ride, I think. Let me just check on the map. Er... Yes. It's called the Jungle River Ride.

Kanako: Let's go on that. There's not much of a queue.

Mike: Before we do that, let's go to the hotel. It's close to here, and I want to check in and put our bags in our room.

Kanako: Right. But after that, let's come straight back here and go on this ride. I really want to try it.

Mike: Sure. I think we should put some waterproof clothes on, though. It looks like the people on the Jungle River Ride are getting soaked. There's a big splash at the end.

Kanako: Good idea. By the way, what shall we do for lunch? I'm feeling quite hungry.

Mike: There's a food court near the hotel. Why don't we eat there after we've checked in and then come back here?

Kanako: That sounds like an excellent plan. This is all so exciting!

1. Where are Kanako and Mike?
   (A) They are in a food court.
   (B) They are at a hotel reception.
   (C) They are waiting in a long line for a ride.
   (D) They are at an amusement park.

2. How many days will Mike and Kanako spend at the amusement park?
   (A) One day
   (B) Two days
   (C) Three days
   (D) One week

3. Why won't Mike and Kanako go on all the roller-coaster rides today?
   (A) Because it's crowded and the queues are too long.
   (B) Because they are too afraid.
   (C) Because the rides aren't running today.
   (D) Because they are too tired and hungry.

4. What day of the week is it?
   (A) Saturday
   (B) Sunday
   (C) Monday
   (D) Tuesday

5. What will Mike and Kanako do next?
   (A) Check in to their hotel
   (B) Have lunch
   (C) Go on the Jungle River Ride
   (D) Buy tickets for all the rides

Ⅲ. Fill in the Gaps

As you listen to the conversation again, fill in each gap with the correct word.

Mike: This is the largest amusement park in the UK, Kanako. Let's look at the map and see where all the best $^{1)}$_____ are.

Kanako: Wow! This park has so much to see and do! How many roller-coaster $^{2)}$_____ are there?

Mike: I think there are five $^{3)}$_____.

Kanako: That many? I want to try them all!

Mike: Me, too. But I don't think we have time to do them all today! The roller-coaster rides are really $^{4)}$_____ and, because it's the weekend, it's really busy today. We're here for two days. We could do the less popular rides today and then do the more popular rides tomorrow. Tomorrow is Monday, so it won't be so crowded.

Kanako: That sounds like a good $^{5)}$_____. Hey, Mike. What's that ride over there? It looks really fun.

Mike: Some sort of river ride, I think. Let me just check on the map. Er... Yes. It's called the Jungle River Ride.

Kanako: Let's go on that. There's not much of a $^{6)}$_____.

Mike: Before we do that, let's go to the hotel. It's close to here, and I want to check in and put our bags in our room.

Kanako: Right. But after that, let's come straight back here and go on this ride. I really want to try it.

Mike: Sure. I think we should put some $^{7)}$_____ clothes on, though. It looks like the people on the Jungle River Ride are getting $^{8)}$_____. There's a big splash at the end.

Kanako: Good idea. By the way, what shall we do for lunch? I'm feeling quite $^{9)}$_____.

Mike: There's a food court near the hotel. Why don't we eat there after we've checked in and then come back here?

Kanako: That sounds like an $^{10)}$_____ plan. This is all so exciting!

IV. Everyday English Phrases

Listen to the audio and write what you hear.

1. ....

2. ....

3. ....

4. ....

V. Incomplete Sentences

Choose the best answer from the two options to complete each sentence below.

1. Japan's amusement parks saw (a decline / an increase) in attendance because of the coronavirus pandemic.

2. Visitors to amusement parks were asked to (train / practice) social distancing and to wear masks.

3. Several popular amusement parks around the globe actually went out of (work / business).

4. Amusement parks must (ready / prepare) for the "new normal"—that is, life with COVID-19.

5. Visitors to theme parks were told to "scream in their hearts, not out (loud / noise)."

VI. Making Sentences

Unscramble the words in the parentheses to make complete English sentences.

1. ここは平日ならそれほど混んでいません。

   _____ ordinary weekdays.

   (won't, on, so, here, it, be, busy)

2. 今日はまだ時間がある。2つ以上の乗り物に行きましょう！

   _____. Let's go on a couple more rides.

   (time, we, today, still, more, some, have)

3. 公園の中に軽食を出すレストランはありますか？

   Are _____ in the park?

   (restaurants, meals, there, any, light, that, serve)

4. 夜は冷えるから上着を着た方がいいね。

   It's _____, so I think we should

   wear our jackets.

   (cold, in, to, be, the, going, evening)

5. 実を言うと、新しいアトラクションにはがっかりしました。

   To tell the truth, _____.

   (new, was, with, I, attractions, the, disappointed)

Coffee Break ☕

間違えやすい英語表現8

学生の皆さんが間違えやすい表現をさらに集めてみました。正しい表現を確認し、繰り返し声に出して練習しましょう。

Incorrect:	I impressed. I bored.
Correct:	I was impressed. I was bored.
Incorrect:	I am busy to study.
Correct:	I am busy studying.
Incorrect:	She is afraid if she will fail.
Correct:	She is afraid she will fail.
Incorrect:	I put on these shoes all day.
Correct:	I wore these shoes all day.
Incorrect:	We went to Asakusa, Ginza, Shinjuku and etc.
Correct:	We went to Asakusa, Ginza, Sinjuku, etc. (and so on.)
Incorrect:	I look forward to see you soon.
Correct:	I look forward to seeing you soon.
Awkward:	The car doesn't move. The trains aren't moving.
Correct:	The car doesn't run. The trains aren't running.

Email

EMAIL MARKETING

I. Before You Listen

Match the words and phrases on the left with their definitions on the right. If you don't know a word's meaning, take a guess.

1. boring ( )   (A) trouble; worry; inconvenience
2. appreciate ( )   (B) to stay in contact or communication with someone far away
3. thoughtful ( )   (C) things and places that are worth seeing
4. bother ( )   (D) to happen to see; notice; catch
5. gigantic ( )   (E) kind; nice; generous
6. sights ( )   (F) to feel thankful; be grateful
7. to keep in touch ( )   (G) not interesting in any way
8. spot ( )   (H) very large; huge; magnificent

Kanako is talking to James after Kanako's return to Japan. Listen to their conversation and then answer the questions that follow.

James: Hi, Kanako. You're back! How was your trip?

Kanako: It was great, thanks. How was your summer vacation?

James: It was a bit boring. I just worked part-time. I didn't go anywhere.

Kanako: Say James, would it be all right if I asked you to do a little favor for me?

James: Anytime, Kanako. What is it?

Kanako: While I was in the UK, I met my British friend Mike. He helped me a lot, so I have written him an email to say how much I appreciate everything he did. Can you read it and check the English for me? Sorry to bother you.

James: No trouble at all. Do you have it now?

Kanako: Yes, I do.

James: Then, why don't you read it to me, and I'll tell you if it sounds OK?

Kanako: OK, here goes. *Hi Mike, I'm writing to say a big thank you for all your help while I was in the UK. Thanks to you, I had a wonderful time. It was very thoughtful of you to meet me at the airport and to take me to so many great places. I particularly enjoyed seeing the tornament at Wimbledon. It was great to see some of my favorite players play in such a big event. Thank you so much for buying the tickets for that day. And thanks also for taking us to the gigantic amusement park. That was a wonderful two days. Anyway, I hope one day you can come to Japan, as I would love to take you to see the sights in my country, too. Please keep in touch, Mike. Best regards, Your friend, Kanako.*

James: That sounds great, Kanako. Mike will be very happy to receive it. Let me just check the spelling for you before you send it. Err.. you've spelled "tournament" wrong. There's a 'u' in it.

Kanako: OK, right. That's a careless error. Thanks for spotting that and for helping me.

1. What did James do in the summer vacation?

    (A) He worked.

    (B) He studied.

    (C) He visited his hometown.

    (D) He took a trip.

2. Who is Kanako writing to?

    (A) James

    (B) Mike

    (C) Kei Nishikori

    (D) Her landlord in the UK

3. What is the main purpose of Kanako's email?

    (A) To express appreciation

    (B) To request information

    (C) To apologize for an error

    (D) To invite a friend to Japan

4. How does James help Kanako?

    (A) He gives her information.

    (B) He writes an email for her.

    (C) He gives her Mike's email address.

    (D) He corrects her English.

5. What's wrong with the email?

    (A) There's a spelling mistake.

    (B) There's a grammar mistake.

    (C) The email is hard to read.

    (D) It's difficult for James to understand.

Ⅲ. Fill in the Gaps

As you listen to the conversation again, fill in each gap with the correct words.

James: Hi, Kanako. You're back! How was your trip?

Kanako: It was great, thanks. How was your summer vacation?

James: It was a bit ¹⁾_____. I just worked part-time. I didn't go anywhere.

Kanako: Say James, would it be all right if I asked you to do a little ²⁾_____ for me?

James: Anytime, Kanako. What is it?

Kanako: While I was in the UK, I met my British friend Mike. He helped me a lot, so I have written him an email to say how much I ³⁾_____ everything he did. Can you read it and ⁴⁾_____ the English for me? Sorry to ⁵⁾_____ you.

James: No trouble at all. Do you have it now?

Kanako: Yes, I do.

James: Then, why don't you read it to me, and I'll tell you if it ⁶⁾_____ OK?

Kanako: OK, here goes. *Hi Mike, I'm writing to say a big thank you for all your help while I was in the UK. Thanks to you, I had a wonderful time. It was very thoughtful of you to meet me at the airport and to take me to so many great places. I ⁷⁾_____ enjoyed seeing the tornament at Wimbledon. It was great to see some of my favorite players play in such a big event. Thank you so much for buying the tickets for that day. And thanks also for taking us to the ⁸⁾_____ amusement park. That was a wonderful two days. Anyway, I hope ⁹⁾_____ day you can come to Japan, as I would ¹⁰⁾_____ to take you to see the ¹¹⁾_____ in my country, too. Please keep in ¹²⁾_____, Mike. Best regards, Your friend, Kanako.*

James: That sounds great, Kanako. Mike will be very happy to receive it. Let me just check the spelling for you before you send it. Err.. you've spelled "tournament" wrong. There's a 'u' in it.

Kanako: OK, right. That's a careless error. Thanks for spotting that and for helping me.

Ⅳ. Everyday English Phrases

 31

Listen to the audio and write what you hear.

1. ....

2. ....

3. ....

4. ....

V. Incomplete Sentences

Choose the word or phrase that best completes each sentence below.

1. In regard to your request, please find (   ) to this email our company catalog.
   (A) stapled   (B) belonging   (C) attached   (D) beside

2. Concerning the above matter, please (   ) that you must make your payment immediately.
   (A) be informed   (B) inform   (C) be informing   (D) let's informed

3. I would like to thank you for sharing (   ) us your invaluable tips on how to write formal emails.
   (A) for   (B) with   (C) about   (D) of

4. Emails have rapidly become the most frequently used means of communication (   ) the world.
   (A) in   (B) through   (C) between   (D) among

5. I apologize for being so careless. I wrote you an email explaining the problem, but then I (   ) to click the "send" icon.
   (A) neglected   (B) decided   (C) avoided   (D) wanted

VI. Making Sentences

Unscramble the words in the parentheses to make complete English sentences.

1. ちょうど昨日、オーストラリアから帰国しました。

   _____ Australia just yesterday.

   (from, I, back, my, to, hometown, came)

2. 過去数週間にわたり、私のためにして下さったことに感謝したいと思います。

   I want to _____ me over the past
   few weeks.

   (you, for, everything, you've, thank, done, for)

3. 旅行中、多くの他の国々を見る機会を持つことができて幸せに思います。

   I _____ to see so many other

   countries on my trip.

   (chance, to, the, have, feel, had, fortunate)

4. ミドルトンさんにくれぐれもよろしくお伝え下さい。

   Please _____.

   (Ms., Middleton, regards, to, kindest, my, give)

5. 近いうちにあなたからまたメールがあるのを楽しみにしています。

   I'm _____ you again soon.

   (from, an, looking, email, receiving, to, forward)

Coffee Break

Thank-you notes

メールや SNS の時代でも、'thank-you notes' や 'bread-and-butter letters' と呼ばれるお礼状は大切です。親切なもてなしや贈り物をもらったときは、後日、あらためて感謝の気持ちを伝えましょう。このような文章に形式的な書き方はありませんが、書き出しや結びの言葉にはいくつか決まった表現があります。

書き出しは Hi Mike, / Dear John, / Dear Professor Martin, などで始め、結びは Your friend, / Sincerely, / Regards, などの結句と自分の名前を記します。また、本文の最後には場合に応じて次のような文を添えると良いでしょう。

Thank you again for the wonderful time.
Take care of yourself and write again soon.
Best regards to your family.
Please say "Hello" to your sister for me.
I hope to hear from you soon.
We can keep in touch by email.

Travel English in Action [B-942]

役に立つ旅行英語

1　刷　2023年4月1日

著　者	バーデン・タイラー	Tyler Burden
	千葉　剛	Tsuyoshi Chiba
	鄭　耀星	Yau-Sin Cheng
	深澤　清	Kiyoshi Fukasawa
	長浜　麻里子	Mariko Nagahama
	福岡　賢昌	Takamasa Fukuoka

発行者　南雲一範　Kazunori Nagumo
発行所　株式会社　南雲堂
　　　　〒162-0801　東京都新宿区山吹町361
　　　　NAN'UN-DO Co., Ltd.
　　　　361 Yamabuki-cho, Shinjuku-ku, Tokyo 162-0801, Japan
　　　　振替口座：00160-0-46863
　　　　TEL: 03-3268-2311（営業部：学校関係）
　　　　　　　03-3268-2384（営業部：書店関係）
　　　　　　　03-3268-2387（編集部）
　　　　FAX: 03-3269-2486

編集者	加藤　敦
表　紙	Nスタジオ
組　版	Office haru
検　印	省　略
コード	ISBN978-4-523-17942-9　C0082

Printed in Japan

E-mail　nanundo@post.email.ne.jp
URL　https://www.nanun-do.co.jp/